California
Native American Tribes

JUANEÑO-LUISEÑO TRIBE

by
Mary Null Boulé

Illustrated by
Daniel Liddell

Merryant Publishers, Inc.
Vashon, WA 98070
206-463-3879

Book Number Nine in a series of twenty-eight

This series is dedicated to Virginia Harding, whose editing expertise and friendship brought this project to fruition.

Library of Congress Catalog Card Number: 92-61897

ISBN: 1-877599-33-6

7615 S.W. 257th St., Vashon, WA 98070.

FOREWORD

Native American people of the United States are often living their lives away from major cities and away from what we call the mainstream of life. It is, then, interesting to learn of the important part these remote tribal members play in our everyday lives.

More than 60% of our foods come from the ancient Native American's diet. Farming methods of today also can be traced back to how tribal women grew crops of corn and grain. Many of our present day ideas of democracy have been taken from tribal governments. Even some 1,500 Native American words are found in our English language today.

Fur traders bought furs from tribal hunters for small amounts of money, sold them to Europeans and Asians for a great deal of money, and became rich. Using their money to buy land and to build office buildings, some traders started business corporations which are now the base of our country's economy.

There has never been enough credit given to these early Americans who took such good care of our country when it was still in their care. The time has come to realize tribal contributions to our society today and to give Native Americans not only the credit, but the respect due them.

Mary Boulé

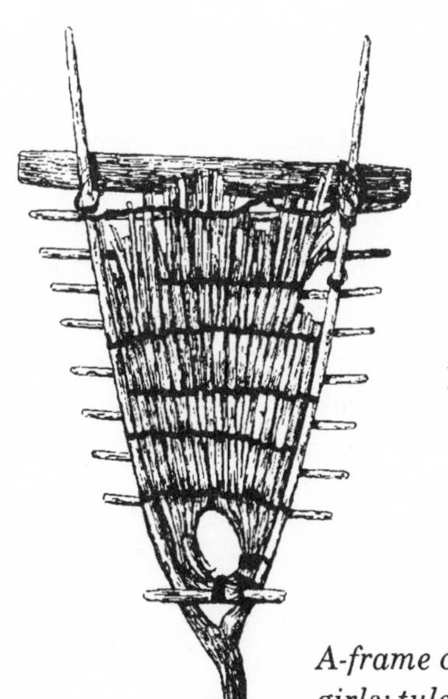

A-frame cradle for girls; tule matting. Tubatulabal tribe.

GENERAL INFORMATION

Creation legends told by today's tribal people speak of how, very long ago, their creator placed them in a territory, where they became caretakers of that land and its animals. None of their ancient legends tells about the first Native Americans coming from another continent.

It is important to respect the different beliefs and theories, to learn from and seek the truth in all of them.

Villagers' tribal history lessons do not agree with the beliefs of anthropologists (scientific historians who study the habits and customs of humans).

Clues found by these scientists lead them to believe that ancient tribespeople came to North America from Asia during the Ice Age period some 20 to 35 thousand years ago. They feel these humans walked over a land strip in the Bering Straits, following animal herds who provided them with food.

Scientists' understanding of ancient people must come from studying clues; for example, tools, utensils, baskets, garbage discoveries, and stories they passed from one generation to the next.

California's Native Americans did not organize into large tribes. Instead they divided into tribelets, sometimes having as many as 250 people. Some tribelets had only one chief for each village.

From 20 to 100 people could be living in one village, which usually had several houses. In most cases, these groups of people were one family and were related to each other. From five to ten people of a family might live in one house. For instance, a mother, a father, two or three children, a grandmother, or aunt or daughter-in-law might live together.

Village members together would own the land important to them for their well-being. Their land might include oak trees with precious acorns, streams and rivers, and plants which were good to eat. Streams and rivers were especially important to a tribe's quality of life. Water drew animals to it; that meant more food for the tribe to eat. Fish were a good source of food, and traveling by boat was often easier than walking long distances. Water was needed in every part of tribal life.

Village and tribelet land was carefully guarded. Each group knew exactly where the boundaries of its land were found. Boundaries were known by landmarks such as mountains or rivers, or they might also be marked by poles planted in the ground. Some boundary lines were marked by rocks, or by objects placed there by tribal members. The size of a territory had to be large enough to supply food to every person living there.

The California tribes spoke many languages. Sometimes villages close together even had a problem understanding one another. This meant that each group had to be sure of the boundaries of other tribes around them when gathering food. It would not be wise to go against the boundaries and the customs of neighbors. The Native Americans found if they respected the boundaries of their neighbors, not so many wars had to be fought. California tribes, in spite of all their differences, were not as warlike as other tribes in our country.

Not only did the California tribes speak different languages, but their members also differed in size. Some tribes were very tall, almost six feet tall. The shortest people came from the Yuki tribe which had territory in what is now Mendocino County. They measured only about 5'2" tall. All Native Americans, regardless of size, had strong, straight black hair and dark brown eyes.

TRADE

Trading between tribes was an important part of life. Inland tribes had large animal hides that coastal tribes wanted. By trading the hides to coastal groups, inland tribes would receive fish and shells, which they in turn wanted. Coastal tribes also wanted minerals and rocks mined in the mountains by inland tribes. Obsidian rock from the northern mountains was especially wanted for arrowheads. There were, as well, several minerals, mined in the inland mountains, which could be made into the colorful body paints needed for religious ceremonies.

Southern tribes particularly wanted steatite from the Gabrielino tribe. Steatite, or soapstone, was a special metal which allowed heat to spread evenly through it. This made it a good choice to be used for cooking pots and flat frying pans. It could be carved into bowls because of its softness and could be decorated by carving designs into it. Steatite came from Catalina Island in the Coastal Gabrielino territory. Gabrielinos found steatite to be a fine trading item to offer for the acorns, deerskins, or obsidian stone they needed.

When people had no items to trade but needed something, they used small strings of shells for money. The small dentalium shells, which came from the far distant Northwest coast, had great value. Strings of dentalia usually served as money in the Northern California tribes, although some dentalia was used in the Central California tribes.

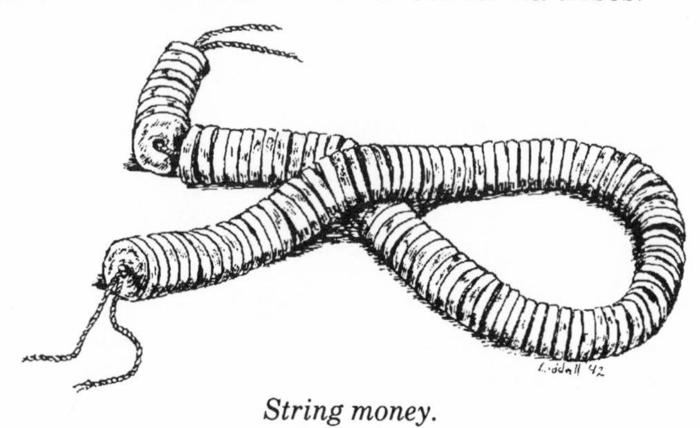

String money.

In southern California clam shells were broken and holes were bored through the center of each piece. Then the pieces were rounded and polished with sandstone and strung into strings for money. These were not thought to be as valuable as dentalia.

Strings of shell money were measured by tattoo marks on the trader's lower arm or hand.

Here is a sample of shell value:

> A house, three strings
> A fishing place, one to three strings
> Land with acorn-bearing oak trees, one to five strings

A great deal of rock and stone was traded among the tribes for making tools. Arrows had to have sharp-edged stone for tips. The best stone for arrow tips was obsidian (volcanic glass) because, when hit properly, it broke off into flakes with very sharp edges. California tribes considered obsidian to be the most valuable rock for trading.

Some tribes had craftsmen who made knives with wooden handles and obsidian blades. Often the handles were decorated with carvings. Such knives were good for trading purposes. Stone mortars and pestles, used by the women for grinding grains into flour, were good trading items.

BASKETS & POTTERY

California tribal women made beautiful baskets. The Pomo and Chumash baskets, what few are left, show us that the women of those tribes might have been some of the finest basketmakers in the world. Baskets were used for gathering and storing food, for carrying babies, and even for hauling water. In emergencies, such as flooding waters, sometimes children, women, and tribal belongings crossed the swollen rivers and streams in huge, woven baskets! Baskets were so tightly woven that not a drop of water could leak from them.

Baskets also made fine cooking pots. Very hot rocks were taken from a fire and tossed around inside baskets with a looped tree branch until food in the basket was cooked.

Most baskets were made to do a certain job, but some baskets were designed for their beauty alone and were excellent for trading. Older women of a tribe would teach young girls how to weave baskets.

Pottery was not used by many California tribes. What little there was seems to have been made by those tribes living near to the Navaho and Mohave tribes of Arizona, and it shows their style. For example, pottery of the California tribes did not have much decoration and was usually a dull red color. Designs were few and always in yellow.

Ohlone hunter wearing deerskin camouflage.

Long thin coils of clay were laid one on top the other. Then the coils were smoothed between a wooden paddle and a small stone to shape the bowl. Pottery from California Native Americans has been described as light weight and brittle (easily broken), probably because of the kind of clay soil found in California.

HUNTING & FISHING

Tribal men spent much of their time making hunting and fishing tools. Bows and arrows were built with great care, to make them shoot as accurately as possible. Carelessly made hunting weapons caused fewer animals to be killed and people then had less food to eat.

Bows made by men of Southern California tribes were made long and narrow. In the northern part of the state bows were a little shorter, thinner, and wider than those of their northern neighbors. Size and thickness of bows depended on the size trees growing in a tribe's territory. The strongest bows were wrapped with sinew, the name given to animal tendons. Sinew is strong and elastic like a rubber band.

Arrows were made in many sizes and shapes, depending on their use. For hunting larger animals, a two-piece arrow was used. The front piece of the arrow shaft was made so that it would remain in the animal, even if the back part was removed or broken off. The arrowhead, or point, was wrapped to the front piece of the shaft. This kind of arrow was also used in wars.

Young boys used a simple wooden arrow with the end sharpened to a point. With this they could hunt small animals like birds and rabbits. The older men of the tribe taught boys how to make their own arrows, how to aim properly, and how to repair broken weapons.

Tribal men spent many hours making and mending fishing nets. The string used in making nets often came from the fibers of plants. These fibers were twisted to make them strong and tough, then knotted into netting. Fences, or weirs, that had one small opening for fish, were built across streams. As the fish swan through the opening they would be caught in netting or harpooned by a waiting fisherman.

Hooks, if used at all, were cut from shells. Mostly hooks could be found when the men fished in large lakes or when catching trout in high mountain areas. Hooks were attached to heavy plant fiber string.

Dip nets, made of netting attached to branches that were bent into a round circle, were used to catch fish swimming near shore. Dip nets had long handles so the fishermen could reach deep into the water.

Sometimes a mild poison was placed on the surface of shallow water. This confused the fish and caused them to float to the surface of the water, where they could be cooped up by a waiting fisherman. Not enough poison was used to make humans ill.

Not all fishing was done from the shore. California tribes used two kinds of boats when fishing. Canoes, dug out of one half a log, were useful for river fishing. These were square at each end, round on the bottom, and very heavy. Some of them were well-finished, often even having a carved seat in them.

Today we think of "balsa" as a very lightweight wood, but in Spanish, the word balsa means "raft". That is why Spanish explorers called the Native American canoes, made from tule reeds, "balsa" boats.

Balsa boats were made of bundled tule reeds and were used throughout most of California. They made into safe, lightweight boats for lake and river use. Usually the balsa canoe had a long, tightly tied bundle of tule for the boat bottom and one bundle for each side of the canoe. The front of the canoe was higher than the back. Balsa boats could be steered with a pole or with a paddle, like a raft.

Men did most of the fishing, women were in charge of gathering grasses, seeds, and acorns for food. After the food was collected, it was either eaten right away or made ready for winter storage.

Except for a few southern groups, California tribes had permanent villages where they lived most of the year. They also had food-gathering places they returned to each year to collect acorns, salt, fish, and other foods not found near their villages.

FOOD

Many different kinds of plant food grew wild in California in the days before white people arrived. Berries and other plant foods grew in the mountains. Forests offered the local tribes everything from pine nuts to animals.

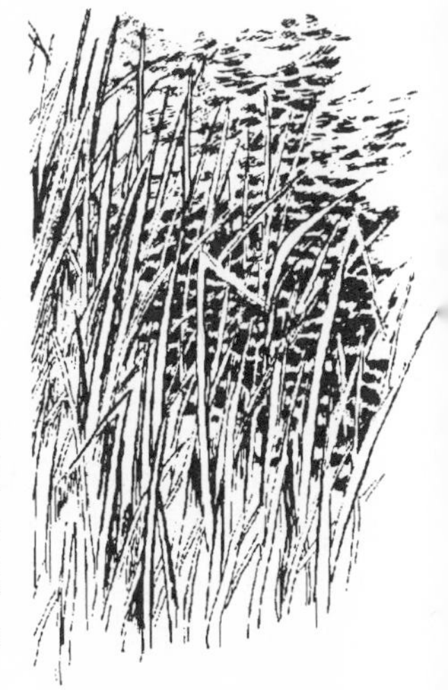

Native Americans found streams full of fish for much of the year. Inland fresh water lakes had large tule reeds growing along their shores. Tule could be eaten as food when plants were young and tender. More important, however, tule was used in making fabric for clothes and for building boats and houses. Tule was probably the most useful plant the California Native Americans found growing wild in their land.

Like all deserts, the one in southern California had little water or fish, but small animals and cactus plants made good food for the local tribes. They moved from place to place harvesting whatever was ripe. Tribal members always knew when and where to find the best food in their territory.

Acorns were the main source of food for all California tribes. Acorn flour was as important to the California Native Americans as wheat is to us today. Five types of California oak trees produced acorns that could be eaten. Those from black oak and tanbark oak seem to have been the favorite kinds.

Since some acorns tasted better than others, the tastiest ones were collected first. If harvest of the favorite acorn was poor some years, then less tasty acorns had to be eaten all winter long.

So important were acorns to California Indians that most tribes built their entire year around them. Acorn harvest marked the beginning of their calendar year. Winter was counted as so many months after acorn harvest, and summer was counted by the number of months before the next acorn harvest.

Acorn harvest ceremonies usually were the biggest events of the year. Most celebrations took place in mid-October and included dancing, feasts, games of chance, and reunions with relatives. Harvest festivals lasted for many days. They were a time of joy for everyone.

The annual acorn gathering lasted two to three weeks. Young boys climbed the oak trees to shake branches; some men used long poles to knock acorns to the ground. Women loaded the nuts into large cone-shaped burden baskets and carried them to a central place where they were put in the sun to dry.

Once the acorns were dried, the women carried them back to the tribe's permanent villages. There they lined special basket-like storage granaries with strong herbs to keep insects away, then stored the acorns inside. Granaries were placed on stilts to keep animals from getting into them and were kept beside tribal houses.

Preparing acorns for each meal was also the women's job. Shells were peeled by hitting the acorns with a stone hammer on an anvil (flat) stone. Meat from the nut was then laid on a stone mortar. A mortar was usually a large stone with a slight dip on its surface. Sometimes the mortar had a bottomless basket, called a hopper, glued to its top. This kept the acorn meat from sliding off the mortar as it was beaten. The meat was then pounded with a long stone pestle. Acorn flour was scraped away from the hopper's sides with a soaproot fiber brush during this process.

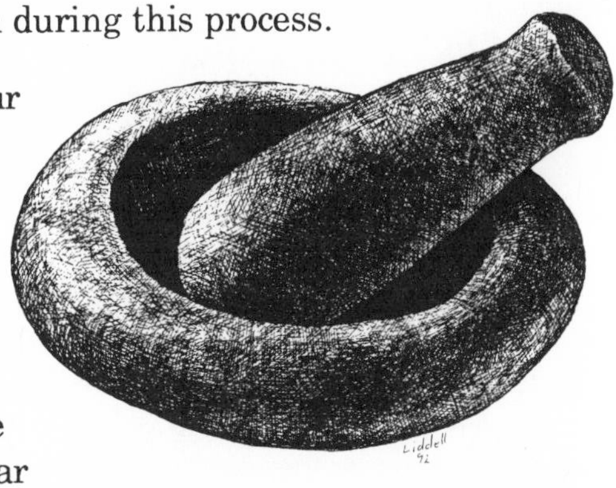

From there the flour was put into an open-worked basket and sifted. A fine flour came through the bottom of the basket, while the larger pieces were put back in the mortar for more pounding.

The most important process came after the acorn flour was sifted. Acorn flour has a very bitter-tasting tannin in it. This bitter taste was removed by a method called leaching. Many tribes leached the flour by first scooping out a hollow in sand near water. The hollow was lined with leaves to keep the flour from washing away. A great deal of hot water was poured through the flour to wash out (leach) the bitterness. Sometimes the flour was put into a basket for the leaching process, instead of using sand and leaves.

Finally the acorn flour was ready to be cooked. To make mush, heated stones were placed in the basket with the flour. A looped tree branch or two long sticks were used to toss the hot rocks around so the basket would not burn. When the mush had boiled, it could be eaten. If the flour and water mixture was baked in an earthen oven, it became a kind of bread. Early explorers wrote that it was very tasty.

Historians have estimated that one family would eat from 1500 to 2000 pounds of acorn flour a year. One reason California native Americans did not have to plant seeds and raise crops was because there were so many acorns for them to harvest each year.

Whether they ate fish or shellfish or plant food or animal meat, nature supplied more than enough food for the Native Americans who lived in California long ago. Many believed their good fortune in having fine weather and plenty to eat came from being good to their gods.

RELIGION

Tribal members had strong beliefs in the power of spirits or gods around them. Each tribe was different, but all felt the importance of never making a spirit angry with them. For that reason a celebration to thank the spirit-gods for treating them well, took place before each food gathering and before each hunting trip, and after each food harvest.

Usually spiritual powers were thought to belong to birds or animals. Most California tribespeople felt bears were very wicked and should not be eaten. But Coyote seems to have been a kind leader who helped them if they were in trouble, even though he seems to have been a bit naughty at times. Eagle was thought to be very powerful and good to native Americans. In some tribes, Eagle was almost as powerful as Sun.

Tribes placed importance on different gods, according to the tribe's needs. Rain gods were the most important spirits to desert tribes. Weather gods, who might bring less rain or warmer temperatures, were important to northern tribes. A great many groups felt there were gods for each of the winds: North, South, East and West. The four directions were usually included in their ceremonial dances and were used as part of the decorations on baskets, pots, and even tools.

Animals were not only worshipped and believed to be spirit-gods, like Deer or Antelope, but tribal members felt there was a personal animal guardian for each one of them. If a tribal member had a deer as guardian, then that person could never kill a deer or eat deer meat.

California Native Americans believed in life after death. This made them very respectful of death and very fearful of angering a dead person. Once someone died, the name of the dead person could never again be said aloud. Since it was easy to accidentally say a name aloud, the name was usually given to a new baby. Then the dead person would not become angry.

Shamans were thought to be the keepers of religious beliefs and to have the ability to talk directly to spirit-gods. It was the job of a village shaman to cure sick people, and to speak to the gods about the needs of the people. Some tribes had several kinds of shamans in one village. One shaman did curing, one scared off evil spirits, while another took care of hunters.

Not all shamans were nice, so people greatly feared their power. However, if shamans had no luck curing sick people or did not bring good luck in hunting, the people could kill them. Most shamans were men, but in a few tribes, women were doctors.

Most California tribal myths have been lost to history because

Religious feather charm.

they were spoken and never written down. The legends were told and retold on winter nights around the home fires. Sadly, these were forgotten after the missionaries brought Christianity to California and moved tribal members into the missions.

A few stories still remain, however, It is thought by historians that northwest California tribes were the only ones not to have a myth on how they were created. They did not feel that the world was made and prepared for human beings. Instead, their few remaining stories usually tell of mountain peaks or rivers in their own territory.

The central California tribes had creation stories of a great flood where there was only water on earth. They tell of how man was made from a bit of mud that a turtle brought up from the bottom of the water.

Many southwest tribes believed there was a time of no sky or water. They told of two clouds appearing which finally became Sky and Earth.

Throughout California, however, all tribes had myths that told of Eagle as the leader, Coyote as chief assistant, and of less powerful spirits like Falcon or Hawk.

Costumes for religious ceremonies often imitated these animals they worshipped or feared. Much time was spent in making the dance costumes as beautiful as possible. Red woodpecker feathers were so brilliant a color they were used to decorate religious headdresses, necklaces, or belts. Deerskin clothing was fringed so shell beads could be attached to each thin strip of leather.

Eagle feathers were felt to be the most sacred of religious objects. Sometimes they were made into whole robes. Usually, though, the feathers were used just for decorations. All these costumes were valuable to the people of each tribe. The village chief was in charge of taking care of the costumes, and there was terrible punishment for stealing them. Clothing worn everyday was not fancy like costuming for rituals.

CLOTHING

Central and southern California's fine weather made regular clothes not really very important to the Native Americans. The children and men went naked most of the year, but most women wore a short apron-like skirt. These skirts were usually made in two pieces, front and back aprons, with fringes cut into the bottom edges. Often the skirt was made from the inner bark of trees, shredded and gathered on a cord. Sometimes the skirt was made from tule or grass.

Willow bark skirt.

In northern California and in rainy or windy weather elsewhere in the state, animal-skin blankets were worn by both men and women. They were used like a cape and wrapped around the body. Sometimes the cape was put over one shoulder and under the other arm, then tied in front. All kinds of skins were used; deer, otter, wildcat, but sea-otter fur was thought to be the best. If the skin was from a small animal, it was cut into strips and woven together into a fabric. At night the cape became a blanket to keep the person warm.

Because of the rainy weather in northern California, the women wore basket caps all the time. Women of the central and south tribes wore caps only when carrying heavy loads, where the forehead had to be used as support. Then a cap helped keep too much weight from being placed on the forehead.

Most California people went barefoot in their villages. For journeys into rough land, going to war, wood gathering, or in colder weather, the tribesmen in central and northwest California wore a one-piece soft shoe with no extra sole, which went high up on the leg.

Southern California tribespeople, however, wore sandals most of the time; wearing high, soled moccasins only when they traveled long distances or into the mountains. Leggings of skin were worn in snow, and moccasins were sometimes lined with grass for more comfort and warmth.

VILLAGE LIFE

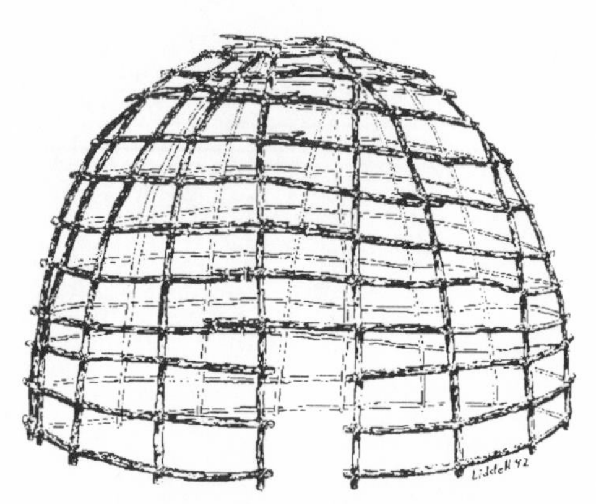

Framework of house – bundles of grass were laid over the framework.

Houses of the California tribes were made of materials found in their area. Usually they were round with domes roofs. Except for a few tribes, a house floor was dug into the earth a few feet. This was wise, for it made the home warmer in winter and cooler in summer. It also meant that less material was needed to make house walls.

Framework for the walls was made from bendable branches tied to support poles. Some frames of the houses were covered with earth and grass. Others were covered with large slabs of redwood or pine bark. Central California villagers made large woven mats of tule reed to cover the tops and sides of houses. In the warmer southern area, brush and smaller pieces of bark were used for house walls.

Most California Native American villages had a building called a sweathouse, where the men could be found when they were not hunting, fishing or traveling. It was a very important place for the men, who used it rather like a clubhouse. They could sweat and then scrape themselves clean with curved ribs of deer. The sweathouse was smaller than a family house. Normally it had a center pole framework with a firepit on the ground next to the pole. When the fire was lit, some smoke was allowed to escape through a hole at the top of the roof; however, most was trapped inside the building. smoke and heat were the main reasons for having a sweathouse. Both were believed to be a way to purify tribal members' bodies. Sweathouse walls were mainly hard-packed earth. The heat produced was not a steam heat but came from a wood-fed fire.

In the center of most villages was a large house that often had no walls, just a roof held up with poles. It was here that religious dances and rituals were held, or visitors were entertained.

Dances were enjoyed and were performed with great skill. Music, usually only rhythm instruments, accompanied the dances. For some reason California Native Americans did not use drums to create rhythms for their dances. Three different kinds of rattles were used by California tribes.

One type, split-clap sticks, created rhythm for dancing. These were usually a length of cane (a hollow stick) split in half lengthwise for about two-thirds of its length. The part still uncut was tightly wound with cord so it would not split all the way. The stick was held at the tied end in one hand and hit against the palm of the other hand to make its sound.

A pebble-filled moth cocoon made rhythm for shaman duties. These could range from calling on spirits to cure illnesses, to performing dances to bring rain. Probably the best sounds to beat rhythm for songs and dances came from bundles of deer hooves tied together on a stick. These rattles have a hollow, warm sound.

The only really "musical" instrument found in California was a flute made of reed that was played by blowing across the edge of one end. Melodies were not played on any of these instruments. Most North American Indians sang their songs rather than playing melodies on music instruments.

Special songs were sung for each event. There were songs for healing sick people, songs for success in hunting, war, or marriage. Women sang acorn-grinding songs and lullabies. Songs were sung in sorrow for the dead and during story-telling times. Group singing, with a leader, was the favorite kind of singing. Most songs were sung by all tribe members, but religious songs had to be sung by a special group. It was important that sacred songs not be changed through the years. If a mistake was made while singing sacred music, the singer could be punished, so only specially trained singers would sing ritual songs.

All songs were very short, some of them only 20 to 30 seconds long. They were made longer by repeating the melodies over and over, or by connecting several songs together. Songs usually told no story, just repeated words or phrases or syllables in patterns.

Song melodies used only one or two notes and harmony was never added. Perhaps that is why mission Indians, at those missions with musician priests, especially loved to sing harmony in the church choirs.

Songs and dances were good methods of passing rich tribal traditions on to the children. It was important to tribal adults that their children understand and love the tribe's heritage.

Children were truly wanted by parents in most tribes and new parents carefully watched their tiny babies day and

Split-stick clapper, rhythm instrument. Hupa tribe.

night, to be sure they stayed warm and dry. Usually a newborn was strapped into a cradle and tied to the mother's back so she could continue to work, yet be near the baby at all times. In some tribes, older children took care of babies of cradle age during the day to give the mother time to do all her work, while grandmothers were often in charge of caring for toddlers.

Children were taught good behavior, traditions, and tribal rules from babyhood, although some tribes were stricter than others. Most of the time parents made their children obey. Young children could be lightly punished, but in many tribes those over six or seven years old were more severely punished if they did not follow the rules.

Just as children do today, Native American youngsters had childhood traditions they followed. For instance, one tribal tradition said that when a baby tooth came out, a child waited until dusk, faced the setting sun and threw the tooth to the west. there is no mention of a generous tooth fairy, however.

Tribal parents were worried that their offspring might not be strong and brave. Some tribes felt one way to make their children stronger was by forcing them to bathe in ice cold water, even in wintertime. Every once in a while, for example, Modoc children were awakened from sleep and taken to a cold lake or stream for a freezing bath.

But if freezing baths at night were hard on young Native Americans, their days were carefree and happy. Children were allowed to play all day, and some tribes felt children did not even have to come to dinner if they didn't want to. In those tribes, children could come to their houses to eat anytime of the day.

The games boys played are not too different from those played today. Swimming, hide and seek among the tule reeds, a form of tetherball with a mud ball tied to a pole, and willow-javelin throwing kept boys busy throughout the day.

Fathers made their sons small bows and arrows, so boys spent much time trying to improve their hunting skills. They practised shooting at frogs or chipmunks. The first animal any boy killed was not touched or eaten by him. Others would carry the kill home to be cooked and eaten by villagers. This tradition taught boys always to share food.

Another hunting tool for boys was a hollowed-out willow branch. this became like a modern day beanshooter, only the Native American boys shot juniper berries instead of beans. Slingshots made good hunting weapons, as well.

Girls and boys shared many games, but girls playing with each other had contests to see who could make a basket the fastest, or they played with dolls made of tule. Together, young boys and girls played a type of ring-around-the-rosie game, climbed mountains, or built mud houses.

As children grew older, the boys followed their fathers and the girls followed their mothers as the adults did their daily work. Children were not trained in the arts of hunting or basketmaking, however, until they became teenagers.

HISTORY

Spanish missionaries, led by Fray Junipero Serra, arrived in California in 1769 to build missions along the coast of California. By 1823, fifty years later, 21 missions had been founded. Almost all of them were very successful, and the Franciscan monks who ran them were proud of how many Native Americans became Christians.

However, all was not as the monks had planned it would be. Native American people had never been around the diseases European white men brought with them. As a result, they had no immunity to such illnesses as measles, small pox, or flu. Too many mission Indians died from white men's diseases.

Historians figure there were 300,000 Native Americans living in California before the missionaries came. The missions show records of 83,000 mission Indians during mission days. By the time the Mexicans took over the missions from the Spanish in 1834, only 20,000 remained alive.

The great California Gold Rush of 1849 was probably another big reason why many of the Native Americans died during that time. White men, staking their claim to tribal lands with gold upon it, thought nothing of killing any California tribesman who tried to keep and protect his territory. 50,000 tribal members died from diseases, bullets, or starvation between the gold Rush Days and 1870. By 1910, only 17,000 California Indians remained.

Although the American government tried to set aside reservations (areas reserved for Native Americans), the land given to the Indians often was not good land. Worse yet, some of the land sacred to tribes, such as burial grounds, was taken over by white people and never given back.

Sadly, mission Indians, when they became Christians, forgot the proud heritage and beliefs they had followed for thousands of years. Many wonderful myths and songs they had passed from one generation to the next, on winter nights so long ago, have been lost forever.

Today some 100,000 people can claim California Native American ancestors, but few pure-blood tribespeople remain. Our link with the Wanderers, who came from Asia so long ago, has been forever broken.

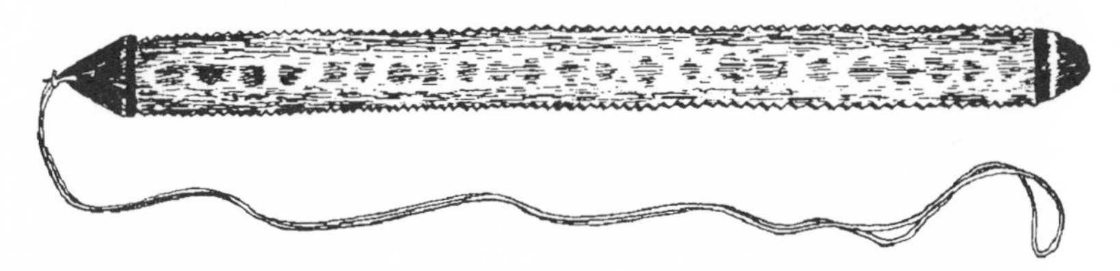

The bullroarer made a deep, loud sound when whirled above the player's head. Tipai tribe.

Villages were usually built beside a lake, stream, or river. Balsa canoes are on the shore. Tule reeds grow along the edge of the water and are drying on poles on the right side of the picture.

Women preparing food in baskets, sit on tule mats. Tule mats are being tied to the willow pole framework of a house being built by one of the men.

LUISEÑO-JUANEÑO TRIBE

As with most California tribes, this group of people probably had no name for itself. The name Luiseño (Loos aye'nyo) was given to those tribal members who became mission Indians at Mission San Luis Rey. Members of the same tribe who became mission Indians at Mission San Juan Capistrano were called Juaneños (Whah neen'yos).

Historians now call both the Juaneño and Luiseño people the "Luiseños". They may have combined the two tribelets under one name because of their being one tribe before mission days. Whatever the reason, the Juaneños still call themselves Juaneño. Today they are a well-organized, active group in and around the city of San Juan Capistrano.

The Juaneño-Luiseño tribe stayed to itself and was not known to be very sociable with nearby tribes. It shared boundaries with the Cupeño, Cahuilla, Gabrielino, and Ipai tribes, and even though they spoke the same language as the neighboring groups, the Juaneño-Luiseños were very careful to protect their privacy. A group of tribal warriors was specially trained to keep other tribes away.

Luiseño-Juaneño territory included most of the land around the San Luis Rey River. It went from the Sierra Santa Ana Mountains in the east to the beach of the Pacific Ocean in the west. Land elevation (height) went from sea level at the beach to 6,000 feet high at Mt. Palomar. More plant and animal life was found in this area than in other parts of Southern California because of climate differences at each elevation.

Summer temperatures in this territory went from the high 60s on the coast to the high 80s inland. Winter temperatures were from the low 50s along the coast to below freezing in the mountains. There was less than 15 inches of rainfall yearly in the coastal region, but 40 inches of rain or snow fell in the mountains each year.

THE VILLAGE

Villages were found in the valleys, beside streams and, along the coast, near mountains. They were usually built in areas protected from wind, near a good supply of water, and in a place safe from attacks by unfriendly neighbors. In the warmer areas, villages had to be built in places shaded from the sun by high slopes of land, such as a canyon.

Villagers owned their own houses, their own small gardens, hunting equipment, trinkets and charms, eagle nests, and songs. Ceremonial houses, granaries for storing food, hunting areas for rabbits and deer, and rock quarries were owned by everyone in the village. The trails and food-gathering campsites also belonged to a tribelet. No people could gather food or hunt on land other than their own without the permission of that land's owners. Trespassing was the main cause of war between tribes or tribelets, so boundaries were carefully marked and guarded.

Most houses were shaped like upside-down ice-cream cones. The ground beneath each house was dug into the earth 12-18 inches. House walls were made of reeds, brush, or bark; whatever was found nearby. Close by, and often attached to the house, was a brush-roofed shelter used for preparing food or making clothes. These shelters were called ramadas, a Spanish word meaning a covering of branches.

The sweathouse was a place where tribal men spent time when they were not hunting or fishing.

Every village had a sweathouse. This was a small building with the floor dug into the earth several inches. It was round and, in prehistoric days (before written history), was covered with earth. A hole at the top let smoke out.

The sweathouse was a place where the men of the village spent their time when they were not hunting or fishing. Fires were built inside the sweathouse and, by using water on hot stones, men would make their bodies sweat. Sweating was thought to purify them, to bring them good luck when hunting. Sweating was also thought to cure a sick person.

In or near the center of a village was a ceremonial building. It was surrounded by a fence, and within the fence, but outside the building, were ground drawings with religious meanings. There was often an altar inside the building which was used for religious ceremonies and rituals.

VILLAGE LIFE

Each village was a group of people usually related on the father's side of the family. The village chief inherited his job from his father or an older relative. He was in charge of the tribelet's religion, the village wealth, and wars. The chief had an assistant who carried out all the leader's orders, as well as important religious duties.

Luiseño-Juaneño people had a much more strict social code than their neighbors. Both tribelets had ruling families who led the villagers, making them obey the strict tribal rules and laws.

People on this council had their own area of knowledge about ritual magic. The chief also chose leaders for rabbit hunts, for fishing trips to the sea, and for deer and antelope hunts. Specialists were even chosen to take care of each of the large food crops, such as acorns, seeds, and cactus plants.

Those on the chief's council inherited their jobs from an older relative. It was up to each council member to train a younger person, usually a talented relative, to take over when that member became too old or ill. Songs, experiences, and how to make fine hunting tools are examples of what was passed on to the trainees by the wise councilmen.

When a child was born, it was the new mother's family who performed birth rituals welcoming the baby. Until it was a few months old, both the new mother and father went on special diets and followed certain tribal laws about what they were allowed to do. Parents felt that following tribal laws would give their child a long and happy life. Babies were loved so much that both new parents gladly did without their favorite foods, or a new father would gladly give up his hunting trips.

As children became teenagers they were honored at ritual ceremonies. At these ceremonies, they were taught to respect older villagers, to listen to what adults had to say, to give older people food, if needed, and not to eat secretly themselves. Teenagers were also taught to keep from getting angry, to be friendly and polite to in-laws when they married, and especially to exactly follow all religious rituals. If young people did not follow the laws, they took the chance of being punished, even killed, by messengers of the god, Chingishngish (Chin gish nish). Those messengers were quite scarey: rattlesnakes, spiders, bears, even sickness!

Boys' ceremonies had dancing, initiation rites, and the teaching of songs and religious rituals. At their ceremonies, girls were given advice on married life and religious rock painting.

Marriages were arranged by the parents, sometimes when a child was born. Because parents made the choice of mates for their children, the marriage was often used as a way to gain more territory, or to make certain families more powerful.

Girls usually were in their early teens when they married. The groom's family gave fine gifts to the bride's family at the marriage ceremony, which was quite fancy. The bride then left her home to live in the groom's village with his family. A divorce was not easy to get, but it was possible, even in those days.

Older men handled ritual ceremonies and made the political decisions for the village. They also taught promising young men how to do their jobs. While younger adult women gathered food and prepared it, the older women stayed at home. They cared for young children, taught the young girls how to baby-sit the smallest children, and how to make clothes and baskets.

Religion played an important part in the villagers' lives, so death was a big concern to them. After the death of a villager, tribal members had to perform up to twelve mourning rituals in a certain order. There was also a ritual washing of the dead person's clothes, followed by a smoking ceremony to purify relatives. The final ceremony was an image-burning, where large dolls were dressed in the dead person's clothes to represent that person to the tribe for one last time. After the ceremony, mourning time was over, and a great feast was held for villagers and relatives from nearby villages. Gifts and food were given to the visiting relatives. When a chief died, there was a special eagle-killing ceremony in his honor.

RELIGION

Religion was so much a part of Luiseño-Juaneño life that some 16 different ritual ceremonies are known to have been celebrated. Among the ceremonies were hunting purification by smoke to bring about a successful hunt, teenage initiations, clothes washing at death and birth, marriage, eagle-feather dances, and peace rituals after a war.

Tribal members felt rituals were important because ritual laws controlled the villagers' actions; they made villagers be kind and law-abiding to those around them. By believing that spirits could hurt them if they did not follow laws, the people behaved better.

It was the tribelet's chief and the shamans who saw to it that laws were obeyed. Men who belonged to secret village clubs, also took care of those who did not obey laws, but it was the shamans who had the most dealings with the villagers.

Luiseño-Juneño man in religious costume. Feathers in skirt are probably condor or eagle feathers. He is holding a basket sieve.

Shamans had objects which they used to reach the spirit gods and to perform their curing and magic spells. Sometimes soapstone or clay pipes were smoked to create the shamans' magic. Mystic power stones of quartz, tourmaline, and other crystals were thought to hold power. Shamans also pretended to swallow long sticks, called swallowing sticks, to impress the people of their tribe. The shamans of their day were much like what we call magicians today, except that most tribal members thought shamans cured sickness.

Rituals were based on tribelet myths, which told of a creator-hero who was the son of Earth Mother. It was this creator-hero who brought all order to the world. When he was killed by those living around him, his death led to the creation of the world of plants, animals, and humans we know today. Luiseños-Juaneños believed that all things on earth were dependent on each other. Therefore, people could not take something from the world around them without replacing what they had taken with a gift of equal value.

The religious beliefs of Luiseños-Juaneños were called Chingichngish. Sand painting was a large part of the rituals of this religion. This tribe's sand paintings are thought by historians to be unchanged since prehistoric days; more so than those of any other southern California tribe.

Each painting was a picture of some part of the universe. For example, some paintings showed the Milky Way and certain parts of the night sky. Some pictured sacred spirit-gods, or human thoughts about their religion. Spirit-gods which brought punishment to those tribal members who did not obey the laws were often drawn in the sand paintings to control the tribe's behavior. These paintings were always destroyed as soon as a ritual was over.

Religious rituals began to die out soon after the explorers discovered the California area; priests of newly founded missions converted many of the Native Americans to Christianity.

FOOD

Juaneño-Luiseño women gathered most plant foods eaten by the tribe, and men usually hunted for animals to be eaten. But sometimes the men helped with the hard jobs of food gathering, such as knocking acorns from oak trees. And once in a while, women hunted and trapped small animals or collected shellfish from the beach. Food was important enough for tribal members to work together for the good of the tribe.

Those tribelets which had villages away from the ocean coastline usually had special food-gathering and fishing sites (places) on the coast. At least once a year, whole villages traveled to these sites. They stayed there for weeks at a time, until enough food could be caught and prepared for the winter months.

Food-gathering trips to the coast were planned to time with low ocean tides. That made clamdigging easier and allowed boat fishing to be closer to shore. Sometimes extra trips were made to the gathering sites if food in storage ran low during January through March. Most gathering sites were found within a day's journey from the permanent village of a tribelet.

Through October and November of each year, the tribelets spent several weeks in the mountain oak tree groves collecting acorns and hunting animals. Acorns were the main food eaten by the tribespeople in this area. There were six kinds of oak trees bearing acorns in the southern California area.

Native Americans liked the taste of some kinds of acorns better than others, gathering as much as they could of their favorite kinds. If not enough of their favorites could be collected, then other less tasty acorns were gathered.

Each tree provided between 160 and 500 pounds of acorns, all of which had to be carried back to the main village and stored in granaries. Huge burden baskets, carried on the women's backs, held the acorns for the trip homeward.

Mostly, the acorn gathering was done on sites owned by a village. Sometimes not enough acorns could be found on its own land to keep the village in food all winter. The leaders then would have to ask another village if its groves could be used. Remember, no tribelet went on another's land without permission.

One of the reasons villages were built near water was because water was needed for acorn leaching. Leaching took out the bitter taste of tannic acid in the nut, and it had to be removed before the mashed nutmeat, called meal, could be cooked. Luiseño-Juaneños used a method called sand-leaching, where a shallow hole was dug into sand and lined with leaves and branches. The meal was placed on top of the liner and hot water poured through it. The women of this tribe were some of the few California Native Americans who used pots, instead of baskets, for cooking acorn meal. In fact, they even had a choice of pots; some were pottery and some were made of steatite, a soapstone mined on Catalina island by the Gabrielino tribe.

Besides acorns, the Luiseño-Juaneños ate many kinds of seeds. Grass, manzanita, sunflower, sage, chia, lemonade berry, wild rose, holly-leaf cherry, prickly pear, and pine-nut seeds were the most important ones. The seeds were dried, ground, and cooked into a mush.

In order to make the plants growing around them produce more seeds, every third year the Luiseño-Juaneños burned their fields with a controlled fire. Tribal members had learned that after a plant is burned, it naturally produced more seeds for a few years. What's more, rabbits could be rounded up and caught with the same fire.

Some plants, such as thistle, white sage, and tree clover, were eaten raw or cooked. Cactus pods and fruits were also eaten. Wild berries, wild grape, and wild strawberries could be eaten raw, or dried for later cooking. Yucca buds, blossoms, and pods were a tasty part of the tribal diet.

In the spring and summer, bulbs, tubers, and roots were dug up for food and usually were eaten fresh. Mushrooms were sometimes found. The women made tea from flowers, fruits, stems, and roots. Some tea was drunk for pleasure, some was used as medicine to cure sickness.

The major animals used for food were deer, jackrabbit, wood rat, mice and ground squirrels, and antelope. Such birds as quail, doves, and ducks also made good food for the tribelet. The tribe did not like to eat tree squirrels, reptiles, or predators like bears, mountain lions, or wolves. No one really knows why they would not eat these animals, but some think it may have been for religious reasons.

From the sea came large sea mammals, such as shark or beached whale, oysters, clams, and fish. Trout and other fresh water fish were found in mountain streams.

Food was cooked in wide-mouthed clay jars over fires, or by wrapping the food in clay or leaves and baking it in an earth oven. Meat was roasted in hot coals or rocks. Seeds were parched (browned) by putting hot rocks into baskets or pottery bowls and tossing them about until the seeds were heated. Tossing the hot stones around not only heated all the seeds, but it kept the rocks from burning the baskets. Food was also cooked with heated rocks or boiled in soapstone pots.

Food was wrapped in leaves or clay before being cooked in the oven.

HUNTING AND FISHING

Deer were stalked either by a group of hunters, or by a single hunter. Most often a hunter wore a deerhead on his own head to keep from being noticed by the animal. The closer a hunter got to his prey, the more accurate his arrows were in killing the animal. If much meat was needed, a group of hunters would chase a herd of deer or antelope into an area where others hunters were waiting to trap and kill them.

Hunters used a shoulder-height bow made of fire-hardened wood. A bow lasted longer if it was not always kept bent by the bowstring; so, hunters learned to string their bows as they ran toward the animal they intended to kill. A fine hunter could string a bow, attach an arrow to it, and shoot all without slowing down.

Sometimes wood-tipped arrows were sharpened to a fine point, then the point was burned just enough to harden the wood.

This kind of all-wood arrow was called a self-arrow. Small boys learned to hunt using the self-arrows by practising their aim on small animals like rabbits or squirrels.

For hunting large animals, adult hunters used arrowheads of felsite or quartz stone. These were attached to the end of arrows with sinew (muscle tendon of animals). Arrows were kept at a hunter's waist in a quiver made of animal hide.

Bows and arrows for fighting wars were mostly the same as those used for hunting, but warriors also used other weapons; some were large and small war clubs, wooden thrusting sticks, lances, and slingshots.

Smaller animals were often killed by a thrown curved stick. This stick was called a boomerang, but it did not return to the person throwing it, like the Australian boomerang.

Throwing stick used for killing small animals. Although curved, it did not return to the thrower, as an Australian boomerang does.

Native Americans also used traps, nets (to catch rabbits and birds), slingshots, and deadfalls to trap smaller animals such as mice. Deadfalls had a heavy stone, or other object placed on top of a lightly propped stick. When an animal hit the stick, knocking it down, the stone would fall on the animal beneath it, killing it.

Fishing done near the ocean shore was from a dugout canoe or a light balsa canoe. Dugouts were made by burning the inside of a log until it was hollow enough to hold people. Only a balsa, or reed, raft was used on inland lakes, or for crossing rivers. If large lakes were nearby, the men needed a more structured boat, which they made from the tule reed. Bundles were tied together to form a boat with points at both ends, with the prow, or front, of the boat higher than the rest. This boat had sides of reed bundles, tightly tied so the boat would not leak, and it was moved and steered by wood paddles.

Juaneño-Luiseños used the same fishing methods as most of the other California tribes. One method was the use of seines, nets made with heavy sinkers on one edge and light floats on the other, so they would hang vertically in the water. Fish traps made of specially woven baskets, dip nets with long wooden handles, and harpoons for huge fish, were also used by tribal fishermen to catch fish.

Like many California tribes, the Juaneño-Luiseños made use of a mild poison to catch fish. Bits of buckeye acorns and/or root of the soap plant were spread across the surface of slow moving pools of water in streams. This poison caused the fish to lose control of their muscles long enough for the fishermen to reach into the water and pick them up, but was not strong enough to hurt humans.

TOOLS AND UTENSILS

Tools were made from anything nature gave the Native Americans. Many of the strongest tools were made of stone, such as pestles used for grinding or pounding, or tools used for flaking crystallized rock into arrowheads. Wood was used for knife handles, for eating spoons, paddles, digging sticks, brushes, or for tongs. Animal antlers were used as wedges to pry things apart. Tiny splintered bird bones and cactus spines became needles for sewing. Rock chips were made into scrappers for removing animal hair from hides. Clamshells, still hinged, made excellent tweezers for the men to pull out their beard hairs.

The women carried cactus pads, or leaves, in nets made from vegetable cords. The nets protected their arms and legs from the plants' sharp needles. Net pouches held food or meat.

Ritual items like pipes were made from clay or soapstone (steatite), which shamans used to purify people of sickness or to ready hunters for hunting trips. Soapstone bowls, used to grind sacred powders and ceremonial blades of obsidian (volcanic glass), were crafted just for religious rituals. There were even specially made baskets that only shamans could use.

Although pottery was sometimes made, baskets were needed and used in every part of tribal life. They were needed to gather and carry food, and to cook and prepare food. Winnowing baskets were shallow trays which helped to remove the outer skins from seeds and grains.

Small baskets became eating bowls, or held ornaments and treasures. Baskets shaped like upside-down ice-cream cones were made to fit on women's backs, so they could haul heavy loads from one place to another. Huge granaries were found in each village. They were made of woven basketry and placed on pole legs to keep animals away from the acorns stored in them. Huge, coarsely woven baskets, some of them three feet high, were made to store blankets, clothing, and ceremonial costumes. Tightly woven baskets carried and stored water. Those not woven tightly enough were sealed with a substance called asphaltum, or tar.

Most pottery was not decorated, but finely coiled baskets were decorated with dark tan, red, or black designs. Three kinds of materials were used in making Luiseño baskets: A grass made the foundation of the basket, and the wrapping material was either a reed or sumach.

To make their small amount of pottery, the paddle and anvil method was used. Clay, made into thick rope-like coils were laid one atop the other. Then the coils were smoothed on the outside with a paddle until the right shape was reached. The pot was then baked in shallow pits dug into the earth. Simple lines were either painted on the surface, or made with the fingernail or a stick to form a design, if any design was put on them at all. Ladies, dippers, bowls of all sizes, and sometimes large jars to hold water were also made of pottery.

Only the California tribes in this most southern part of California seem to have made pottery. Anthropologists think that the art of making pottery came from tribes over in

Arizona and New Mexico. These tribes might have moved to the west coast a long time ago, bringing the process with them. Or they could have traded with the California tribes, teaching them how to make their own pottery. The clay soil of California is not the right kind to make such sturdy pottery as found in Arizona.

CLOTHING

Clothing was not very important to the southern California tribes. The climate was mostly warm, except for a few weeks or months in winter. Men and children seldom wore any clothes. Women wore woven cedar-bark double aprons which looked like skirts.

If the weather did get cool, tribal members wore cloaks and robes made from deer-, otter-, or rabbit-skin strips wound on lengths of vegetable-fiber cord. The strips were actually woven together. These cloaks served as blankets on cool nights, as well. Sandals, if they were worn at all, were of yucca fiber. Some Luiseños wore deerskin moccasins when they traveled long distances.

Although they wore little clothing, the Juaneño-Luiseño people did wear body ornaments. Ornaments made of clay, bone, stone, shell, bear claws, and other objects from nature hung from ears, noses, or necklaces. Anklets and bracelets were made from human hair. Beads or pendants were crafted from sheets of mica (fool's gold), deer hooves, bear claws, and abalone shells. Men liked ear and nose ornaments of cane or bone, sometimes adding beads.

Certain stones were thought to be of great value as ornaments. Especially liked were quartz, garnet, opal, topaz, agate, and jasper.

Body painting for men and women, and tattooing for men, usually had to do with religious ceremonies. Costumes for religious ceremonies were colorful and pretty. Men wore eagle-feather headdresses. Owl- or raven-feather plumes were worn on the head or held in the hands. Dancers wore colorful skirts and shoulder bands.

MUSIC AND GAMES

Some tribes in California did not put much importance on music, but to the Luiseño-Juaneño people it was so important that songs, especially religious songs, were considered owned by the person who wrote them. The only way a tribal member could sing another person's song was if the member had inherited the song when the composer died.

Music used in religious ceremonies had to be sung exactly right, or it was feared that spirit-gods would punish the singer who made a mistake. Needless to say, songs were practised very well before a ceremony.

Only one musical instrument played the melody of a song, and that was a simple flute made of cane (a hollow stem) with holes drilled along its side. The rest of the instruments were used for keeping the beat, or rhythm. Tiny bird bones and smaller cane were made into whistles. Split-stick clappers were hit onto the palms of the players' hands, or were shaken.

Split stick clapper, rhythm instrument.

There were rattles of turtle shell, gourd, or deer hooves. Deer hooves, when hollowed, were actually used by all the Native American tribes in our country. Luiseño-Juaneños used deer hoof rattles to call to spirit-gods for good luck in hunting and for ceremonies mourning those who had died.

One very strange sounding instrument used in ritual songs was the bull-roarer. It was a flat piece of board with a strong string tied through a hole at one end. A player would hold very tightly to the dangling end of the string. The board was swung around in a circle over the player's head. The bull-roarer made a loud humming sound that some people thought sounded like thunder. It had an eerie sound, so was considered by Juaneño-Luiseños to be a most sacred instrument and was used in rituals. The bull-roarer was also used to call people to religious events because it made such a loud noise.

All tribes had games they played just for fun. Luiseños had a team game they called peon which they enjoyed a great deal. It used bone and wood cylinders and had counters to keep track of scores. Dice were made and used in several games of chance. All California Native Americans liked games of chance, or gambling, to help pass the time during long winter days.

Games using wooden balls, like field hockey, were played on outdoor fields. In one exciting game of skill, players tried to throw sticks through rolling rings or hoops. Acorn tops were needed for some games, and children played games with strings that were much like the cat's cradle children play today.

HISTORY

European explorers had watched the Juaneño-Luiseño people for years before they spoke with the tribe. The first Europeans who tried to speak to them were members of the Gaspar de Portola expedition. This group of explorers was a part of the mission expedition sent by Spain to begin building the California missions. Their leader was the Francescan monk, Fray Junipero Serra.

By 1800 there were four missions built in the southern part of what would become California: San Diego, San Luis Rey, San Juan Capistrano, and San Gabriel. Historians guess there were about fifty Luiseño villages at that time, with perhaps 10,000 tribal members living there. No sooner had the Europeans arrived, than the Native Americans started coming down with white man's diseases. Small pox, scarlet fever, chicken pox, and especially measles were deadly to the Luiseño-Juaneño people because they had never been around such diseases before. Thousands became sick and died.

As more and more tribal members moved into the missions, becoming what we call mission Indians, the more they died of white men's sicknesses.

The Luiseño-Juaneño people became mission Indians at both Mission San Juan Capistrano and Mission San Luis Rey. At Mission San Luis Rey, the priest in charge was Fr. Peyri. He chose to let most mission Indians live in their own villages. He took the church's religious services to the villages, supervising the planting of mission fields around each village when he visited. This allowed tribal members to continue eating the same tribal foods they always had, and tribelet leaders were even permitted to be in charge of village life. Most missions made their mission Indians live just outside the mission walls, away from their villages.

Among other things, Indian mission workers were taught the Spanish language; farming skills, such as how to raise cattle and sheep; carpentry; the making of adobe brick; and Christianity. Sadly, however, the Native Americans kept dying from diseases the European people brought with them from Spain.

In 1834, when Mexico drove Spanish missionaries and soldiers out of California and took over the missions, the mission Indians were turned into slaves for wealthy Mexican landowners. Mission lands, which had been promised to them by Spanish missionaries, were taken by Mexicans instead. The tribe organized revolts and uprisings against the Mexicans. Many former tribal members ran away from the mission and became members of the inland tribelets.

Those mission Indians that stayed became a part of Mexican city life. Some even bought land in the Temecula, La Jolla, and Kuka areas. Most tribal villages continued to survive and added farming to their lives. By 1860 only 1,120

Luiseño-Juaneños were left, according to census records.

Unfortunately, when California became United States property, the federal government took tribal lands away from the tribelets. Fights began to break out between the white settlers given tribal land and the remaining Luiseños-Juaneños. In 1875, reservation land was given to the tribe that included the villages of Pala, Potrero, La Jolla, and Tapiche. The settlement of Pala can be found near San Diego today.

With the forming of the reservation, the federal government was at once in charge of every part of Indian life. Law courts, schools, health care, and policemen, were all handled by government people. Trouble was never far away from the tribe. The government did not really understand the tribe's wants and needs, and yet the tribal members were not allowed to make their own decisions about those needs. Fortunately, through all the hard times, Luiseño-Juaneños continued to support themselves by farming and ranching.

Many tribal men joined the army in World War I. When they came home in the early 1920s, they used the newly learned skills from their army days and began to earn more money. By the 1950s, the tribes began to take over leadership of the reservation, leaving only the legal work concerning land to be handled by the United States government.

In the 1960s, the government started paying for programs to build low-cost housing and to pay for job training. Since these kinds of programs could be funded only if a large amount of people would receive help, the Luiseño-Juaneño people met with other Native American tribes and organized themselves into one larger group of California Native Americans.

More than most other southern California tribes, this tribe seems to have become a working force in the California Intertribal Council, the main council representing Native Americans in Washington, D.C. today.

In 1970 about one third of the Luiseño-Juaneños lived on

reservations at La Jolla, Rincon, Pala, and a few other places. The rest of the tribal members lived within twenty miles of a reservation. Many of the them are trained electricians, carpenters, ranchers, farmers, and the like. Some tribal members are teachers, professors, engineers, and other professionals.

Luiseño-Juaneños have their own programs for caring for senior citizens and homeless people. They are busy planning improved housing and developing the natural resources of their land.

Much of the old culture is still around today. Certain beliefs about life and behavior have not changed. Even some religious rituals and the use of shamans continue. Ceremonies still are held at the installing of new chiefs and at funerals.

Tribal language is still spoken by some of the older people. Young people of the tribe are beginning to show enough interest in the original language so that classes have been formed to teach the language. Interest is also shown in learning nonreligious songs and dances. Tribal foods, such as acorns, yucca, and wild animal meats are still eaten. Some of the original herbal medicines and curing methods can be found today in Luiseño and Juaneño homes.

Fiestas, like those held in mission days, are still celebrated several weekends a year. One favorite game, a guessing game called Peon, is still played at fiestas. Both men and women make up the team players, and it is a great honor to play well.

Perhaps it was the fact that the first Mission Luis Rey priest, Fr. Pyri, allowed the Luiseños to live in their own villages two hundred years ago. Or it might be because the Luiseño-Juaneño tribelets taught their people to follow tribal laws with great care. Whatever the reasons, the Luiseño-Juaneño people have managed to keep much of what was important to their prehistoric ancestors (relatives who lived long ago) as the important things in their lives today.

JUANEÑO - LUISEÑO TRIBE OUTLINE

I. Introduction
  A. Explaining tribal names
  B. Territory boundaries
  C. Climate, temperatures and rainfall
II. The village
  A. Reasons for location of village
  B. Ownership of property
    1. Private ownership
    2. Village ownership
    3. Trespassing
  C. Houses
    1. Description
    2. Materials used
  D. Sweathouse
  E. Ceremonial house
III. Village life
  A. Relationship of tribal people
  B. Village chief
    1. Assistants and council
  C. Childbirth customs
  D. Teenage rituals
  E. Marriage rules and customs
  F. Death customs
IV. Religion
  A. Ritual ceremonies
  B. Shamans
  C. Myths and sand paintings
V. Food
  A. Gathering jobs of tribe
  B. Gathering sites
    1. Coastal sites
    2. Mountain sites
  C. Acorns
    1. Gathering
    2. Preparations

D. Plant foods
1. Seeds, berries, cactus
2. Burning of fields
E. Animals
VI. Hunting and fishing
A. Hunting methods
1. Stalking and group hunts
2. Bows and arrows, throwing sticks
3. Traps and nets
B. Fishing methods
1. Balsa and dugout canoes
2. Nets, traps, harpoons, and poison
VII. Tools and utensils
A. Objects from nature
1. Stone
2. Wood
3. Bone
4. Steatite
B. Pottery
VIII. Clothing
A. Men and children
B. Women
C. Cool weather clothes
D. Body ornaments and painting
IX. Music and games
A. Music
1. Songs
2. Instruments
B. Games
1. Indoor games
2. Outdoor games
X. History
A. Before missions
B. Mission days
1. White man's diseases
2. Life at Mission San Luis Rey

C. Mexican take-over of missions

D. United States takes away tribal land

    1. Pala today

E. Indian reservations

F. Tribal leadership begins

G. Juaneño-Luiseños today

    1. Active in Indian Councils
    2. Language
    3. Fiestas

GLOSSARY

AWL: a sharp, pointed tool used for making small holes in leather or wood

CEREMONY: a meeting of people to perform formal rituals for a special reason; like an awards ceremony to hand out trophies to those who earned honors

CHERT: rock which can be chipped off, or flaked, into pieces with sharp edges

COILED: a way of weaving baskets which looks like the basket is made of rope coils woven together

DIAMETER: the length of a straight line through the center of a circle

DOWN: soft, fluffy feathers

DROUGHT: a long period of time without water

DWELLING: a building where people live

FLETCHING: attaching feathers to the back end of an arrow to make the arrow travel in a straight line

GILL NET: a flat net hanging vertically in water to catch fish by their heads and gills

GRANARIES: basket-type storehouses for grains and nuts

HERITAGE: something passed down to people from their long-ago relatives

LEACHING: washing away a bitter taste by pouring water through foods like acorn meal

MORTAR: flat surface of wood or stone used for the grinding of grains or herbs with a pestle

PARCHING: to toast or shrivel with dry heat

PESTLE: a small stone club used to mash, pound, or grind in a mortar

PINOLE: flour made from ground corn

INDIAN RESERVATION: land set aside for Native Americans by the United States government

RITUAL: a ceremony that is always performed the same way

SEINE NET: a net which hangs vertically in the water, encircling and trapping fish when it is pulled together

SHAMAN: tribal religious men or women who use magic to cure illness and speak to spirit-gods

SINEW: stretchy animal tendons

STEATITE: a soft stone (soapstone) mined on Catalina Island by the Gabrielino tribe; used for cooking pots and bowls

TABOO: something a person is forbidden to do

TERRITORY: land owned by someone or by a group of people

TRADITION: the handing down of customs, rituals, and belief, by word of mouth or example, from generation to generation

TREE PITCH: a sticky substance found on evergreen tree bark

TWINING: a method of weaving baskets by twisting fibers, rather than coiling them around a support fiber

NATIVE AMERICAN WORDS WE KNOW AND USE

PLANTS AND TREES
hickory
pecan
yucca
mesquite
saguaro

ANIMALS
caribou
chipmunk
cougar
jaguar
opossum
moose

STATES
Dakota – friend
Ohio – good river
Minnesota – waters that reflect the sky
Oregon – beautiful water
Nebraska – flat water
Arizona
Texas

FOODS
avocado
hominy
maize (corn)
persimmon
tapioca
succotash

GEOGRAPHY
bayou – marshy body of water
savannah – grassy plain
pasadena – valley

WEATHER
blizzard
Chinook (warm, dry wind)

FURNITURE
hammock

HOUSE
wigwam
wickiup
tepee
igloo

INVENTIONS
toboggan

BOATS
canoe
kayak

OTHER WORDS
caucus – group meeting
mugwump – loner politician
squaw – woman
papoose – baby

CLOTHING
moccasin
parka
mukluk – slipper
poncho

BIBLIOGRAPHY

Cressman, L. S. *Prehistory of the Far West.* Salt Lake City, Utah: University of Utah Press, 1977.

Heizer, Robert F., volume editor. *Handbook of North American Indians; California, volume 8.* Washington, D.C.: Smithsonian Institute, 1978.

Heizer, Robert F. and Elsasser, Albert B. *The Natural World of the California Indians.* Berkeley and Los Angeles, CA; London, England: University of California Press, 1980.

Heizer, Robert F. and Whipple, M.A.. *The California Indians.* Berkeley and Los Angeles, CA; London, England: University of California Press, 1971.

Heuser, Iva. *California Indians.* PO Box 352, Camino, CA 95709: Sierra Media Systems, 1977.

Macfarlen, Allen and Paulette. *Handbook of American Indian Games.* 31 E. 2nd Street, Mineola, N.Y. 11501: Dover Publications, 1985.

Murphey, Edith Van Allen. *Indian Uses of Native Plants.* 603 W. Perkins Street, Ukiah, CA 95482: Mendocino County Historical Society, © renewal, 1987.

National Geographic Society. *The World of American Indians.* Washington, DC: National Geographic Society reprint, 1989.

Tunis, Edwin. *Indians.* 2231 West 110th Street, Cleveland, OH: The World Publishing Company, 1959.

Weatherford, Jack. *Native Roots.* 201 E. 50th Street, New York, NY 10022: Crown Publishers, 1991.

Credits:
The Pollard Group, Inc., Tacoma, Washington 98409
Dona McAdam, Mac on the Hill, Seattle, Washington 98109

Acknowledgements:
Richard Buchen, Research Librarian, Braun Library,
Southwest Museum